Kevin Kutz's
Lincoln Highway

SEE 3 STATES AND 7 CO...

SHIP
HOTEL·RESTAURANT

That S.S. Grand View—Ship Hotel· Not a finer place could anyone sell· Moonshine in Quart Bottles·...

S.S. GRANDVIEW
SHIP HOTEL.
opened 1932

Kevin Kutz's
Lincoln Highway

Kevin Kutz

Foreword by
Brian Butko

Introduction by
Mary Thomas
Pittsburgh Post-Gazette Art Critic

STACKPOLE
BOOKS

Published by
STACKPOLE BOOKS
5067 Ritter Road
Mechanicsburg, PA 17055
www.stackpolebooks.com

Printed in China
10 9 8 7 6 5 4 3 2 1
FIRST EDITION

EDITOR: *Kyle Weaver*
DESIGNER: *Beth Oberholtzer*

PAINTING PHOTOGRAPHY:
Richard Stoner, 22, 45, 57, 65, 83, 109
Bob Webb, 99
Randy Williams, 12–13

Frontispiece:

Ship Hotel

1995, watercolor, 28 x 32 inches
Collection of Bill and Julie Miller

Library of Congress Cataloging-in-Publication Data

Kutz, Kevin.
     [Lincoln highway]
     Kevin Kutz's Lincoln highway / Kevin Kutz ; foreword by Brian Butko ; introduction by
Mary Thomas.— 1st ed.
          p.   cm.
     Includes index.
     ISBN-13: 978-0-8117-3264-2 (papberback)
     ISBN-10: 0-8117-3264-9 (pbk.)
     1. Kutz, Kevin—Themes, motives.   2. Lincoln Highway—In art.   3. Pennsylvania—
In art.   I. Title.
ND237.K92A4   2006
759.13—dc22
                                                                    2005024734

Foreword

In 1989, the Society for Commercial Archeology (SCA) held its first photo contest, hoping to encourage documentation of the roadside landscape. Tourist cabins, drive-in theaters, and a few roadside giants were among the many subjects captured on film. Thirty-six of the entries, including the winners, were enlarged, matted, and framed and began traveling to venues around the country. I helped bring them to Pittsburgh, where one visitor looked around and then thoughtfully proclaimed, "This is exactly the kind of trash we're trying to keep *out* of our town."

Many people do not consider roadside relics as trash, but it's likely that many just never consider these things *at all*. We may stay in a motel, gas up at a station in the morning, and grab a quick lunch at a diner, but how many of us take photos of these places, how many care or even notice when one of them disappears?

Critics have long called for the roadscape to be cleansed of billboards and junkyards, but the pace accelerated in the 1960s, as four-lane highways and suburban sprawl spread growth farther and faster than ever. Artists, always a few steps ahead of the populace, began to photograph and paint the previous generation's roadside architecture, which fit perfectly the era's fascination with its own pop culture.

By the 1970s, a few books were spreading the gospel of two-lane roads and the attractions along them, but they were speaking to a fringe audience. When the SCA was founded in 1977, canopy gas stations and shoe-shaped houses were considered unworthy of preservation or even discussion. They were mostly an embarrassment to the owners, and townspeople wanted a new McDonald's, not an old, funny-shaped building. Even by 1990, when the above "trash" comment was made, the roadside fan base was limited. I remember well how "diner" equaled "greasy spoon," so much so that decades-old diners were being rethemed and renamed as "family restaurants."

Perhaps the biggest force for change was the Internet. Scattered and disparate groups—hot rodders, family vacationers, and people who just like an old café or mom-and-pop motel—found kindred souls across the country. Newspapers had already been running stories when a town's last diner or drive-in closed; now journalists could make a living writing nostalgic on-the-road pieces.

The Lincoln Highway followed just this trajectory. It had once been the most famous road in the world, praised by road planners and those with wanderlust the world over. The rise of federal highways in the 1920s and Interstates in the 1950s left it mostly forgotten, however, its original route lost to bypasses, its founders a footnote to history.

But readers of early roadside books would have noticed the road in John Baeder's moving 1982 book, *Gas, Food, and Lodging*. He reminded us of the joys of early highways and the places waiting to be discovered, such as Pennsylvania's Ship Hotel. One of his fun stories was about the Coffee Pot and Dunkle's Gulf in Bedford. When a local artist heard that John couldn't find the pot, he wrote him about how he often set up his easel to paint it, only to be laughed at by locals.

A quarter century later, awareness and appreciation of the American roadside are much greater, thanks to books like Baeder's and artists such as the one who wrote to him, Kevin Kutz. Today no one is laughing.

Brian Butko

Preface

More than twenty years ago, it dawned on me that several of the paint sites that I was working from were along the same road. I wondered what else was out there and the exploration began. For a few years, I painted dozens of Lincoln Highway subjects. I then began to stray away onto other roads, almost feeling a little unfaithful. But I keep coming back to the Lincoln, and this book represents more than twenty-five years of my paintings of the road.

Kyle Weaver, Stackpole Books editor and Lincoln Highway fan, had the patience, perseverance, and encouragement that made this project come to fruition. His insight to make an art/history book appealed to this painter who happens to be a history buff. Out of the thousands of paintings I've done so far, we rounded up about eighty to include in this collection.

I believe in my heart that the celebration of American icons such as the Lincoln Highway is a pure enough form of patriotism, without the flutes and flags. These paintings were not done for stock. They are more than mere depictions of quaint old gas stations with old automobiles out-side. The celebration of our past and present will transport us into the future one day at a time. That's the way it is and always has been. A film-maker is making a movie along the Lincoln, and Brian Butko recently completed his coast-to-coast book on the subject, *Greetings from the Lincoln Highway*. Many of the places have gone by the wayside, but over time I came to feel that the old Lincoln Highway will always be a brother to me. There's really not an end—chances are that many of us today will get in our cars, be on our way, and see the road in a different light.

Most of the artists I have run across who deal with such subjects as movie theaters, gas stations, restaurants, diners, and motels are photo-realists. I'm kind of an idiosyncrasy, working in the manner of artists a hundred years ago, painting outdoors (plein aire) and using the impressionists' technique.

How did I get to this point? I spent most of my school years looking out the windows, and while in art school I skipped classes to wander around Pittsburgh and draw in my sketchbooks. I finally realized it was costing my parents a lot of money for professors to tell me to paint when I was going to do it anyway, so I left art school. A few years later, I slept in a tent along the ocean in Connecticut and painted during the daylight hours under the direction of eighty-one-year-old master Robert Brackman. He had been a student of Robert Henri and George Bellows of the Ash Can School. Color became my focus through his teaching and has remained my main intrigue. After my brief art school training and being influenced by hundreds of artists, mostly through viewing their works in museums up and down the East Coast, I have thrown everything into the pot to define my artwork. My mentors, whom I have met or corresponded with through the years, include Raphael Soyer, Jack Levine, Henry Koerner, Ivan Albright, John Baeder, Wolf Kahn, John Margolies, and Jerome Witkin. A good many Pittsburgh artists—Robert Qualters, Sam Rosenberg, Herbert Olds, Douglas Wilson, "Wild" Willie Patterson, Charlie Pitcher, Barbara Mitchell, Chuck Olson, Charles "Bud" Gibbons, and Charlie Jackson—have inspired and encouraged me as well.

Kevin Kutz

Introduction

Mary Thomas

As it crosses the fertile fields of eastern Pennsylvania, toils up the steep slopes of the great Appalachian chain, and rolls through the river valleys in the west, the Lincoln Highway carries with it the history of the state, its land, and its people.

For most, the road is a conduit from one place to another, the landscape barely noticeable in the fleeting frames of modern travel. But for a gifted few who take the time to look and listen, it is a storyteller of profound dimension, its endlessly fascinating revelations infused with humor, drama, and insight.

Kevin Kutz is one of those few. And his acute impressionistic paintings are a visual record of that history, reinterpreted through memory and the hand of the artist, a combination of lore and fact, folk and sophisticate, ideal and actual.

Art styles pass in and out of fashion—consider the shaky course that figurative representation has wandered over the last century—and in contemporary times, it has become a common practice to disparage art designated within the broad label "regional." The argument is that only in great urban centers do au courant conversations about art and culture occur, and that elite dialogue drives the artistic expression that will edify and codify the times.

The notion is only partially correct, because it represents only part of the picture. Working at

Kevin Kutz, 2005.

times in opposition and at other times in complementary balance are the concerns and rhythms of the rest of the country, particularly true of a nation as diverse in geography and population, as large in size, as the United States.

Kutz is one of the weights on the rural side of the scale. If rapidity, change, variety, and cosmopolitanism characterize the city, the hinterland may be seen as measured, stable, homogenous, and retaining identity.

This is apparent in the artist's subject matter but is also present in the way he doggedly pursues, interprets, and depicts his material. The complex and compelling story of place that Kutz unfolds is not the result of a quick pass, but of a persistent fascination with the monumental, the minutiae, and whatever falls between that constitute the geography he treads with the regularity of breath.

When Kutz paints a landscape of rolling fields and forested hills, he captures the essence of central Pennsylvania, where his home, Bedford, is located, and which he's painted throughout his career. This is not necessarily achieved by making the scene representational. Kutz isn't wedded to the exact curve of a hill, configuration of trees, or distribution of color that lie before him. Rather, it is his cultivated knowledge of the genius loci of his home turf that allows him not only to very capably paint what a visitor may see, if he so chooses, but also to enlarge upon that reality to convey a greater, underlying concept.

It seems evident from the numbers of paintings and drawings that he's done, as well as their evolution, variance, and content, that Kutz returns to site to paint with questions on his mind. "Why is this significant?" he seems to be asking. "Where did it come from? What preceded it? What happened in that spot? Who passed by here?" Or maybe the musings are of a personal nature: "What is it that draws me back?" This adds dimensionality to Kutz's already exceptional paintings.

Like the Impressionist masters of the late nineteenth century, Kutz paints outdoors, or plein air, and also like them, his realism is poeticized. His palette is intense, his paint application tactile; when it suits him, he distributes color like thrown confetti. He is in full control of his brush, which is at times vibrant with short, confident strokes that activate the canvas in an expressionistic manner.

But there is more to these paintings than their sensual, formal quality.

Kutz treats space as a signifier. Through use of cropping, dramatic perspectives, nontraditional angles, and long views or close-ups, he instills in his subjects political, societal, psychological, and metaphysical underpinnings.

Stretches of empty road that snake through farmland speak of man's harmonious residency on the land, but also suggest his intrusion, in the way that agricultural scenes painted by nineteenth-century American artists foretold the dissolution of the natural environment that was so significant to the identity of the young nation. Kutz also has blatantly relayed this latter sentiment, as in his painting titled *Incoming McMansions*, which was exhibited in 2003 at the Southern Alleghenies Musuem of Art and showed subdivisions encroaching on the fields.

The breadth of his subject matter—from the lonely long view that recalls expanses of virgin wilderness to a close-in of a long-inhabited street —suggests a reconnoiterer, constantly absorbing what's before him and folding it into the mix.

This somewhat analytical gather is consistently and attentively bent through the prism of Kutz's aesthetic, and when a component of it steps out of his mind and onto the canvas, what in some hands could be as dry and predictable as census data instead radiates vitality. The accomplishment here is that this is not an imposed, generic brightness consciously constructed of color and line to evoke mood. Kutz infuses his Lincoln Highway paintings with a life force derived from merging his own significant sensitivities with the spirit that resides within his subjects, which is what seduced him in the first place. It is a vividness born of passion discovered and passion released. And it is the common denominator in these works, which vary from celebratory to elegiac, wondrous to melancholic.

His inclusivity extends to, among others, highway workers, farmers, and obliquely, the ghosts of the engineers responsible for generally unheralded monuments like bridges, from diners to drive-ins to the characteristic roll of a Pennsylvania hillock or the sculpted shadow cast by a bank of snow.

Portraits of quirky roadside attractions built in the early decades of the last century pay homage to eclecticism and Yankee ingenuity. They also indicate Kutz's affection for such individualistic expression, and his committing them to canvas is his way of both honoring them and quietly soliciting appreciation for and protection of them.

Unlike some artists and photographers, Kutz is not a detached onlooker. When one of his often-visited subjects—a small building shaped like a coffee pot that began catching the eyes of drivers approaching Bedford in 1925—appeared to be on the road to ruin, he joined preservationists who were speaking out in favor of its rescue. A bittersweet painting shows the Coffee Pot, aged and peeling, being moved on a gloomy day to the Bedford County Fairgrounds, where it was to be restored and eventually reopened in some capacity.

Another favorite of his didn't fare as well. Built to resemble a large ship, and propped on the side of a mountain like Noah's Ark come to rest, the imaginative Ship Hotel pulled in travelers on the descent who wanted to experience the magnificent view of three states from its deck, as well as those whose automobiles benefited from a stop after ascending the steep approach from the east. The diversion of traffic from the old route by the completed Pennsylvania Turnpike, the updated engineering of cars, and changing tastes cut into the number of patrons it served, and after various failed attempts to reinvigorate it, the hotel burned to the ground in 2001.

That was an obvious blow to Kutz, who had painted it frequently and from numerous vantage points. *Grand View Ship Hotel*, a memorable image from 1985 in the permanent collection of the Westmoreland Museum of American Art, Greensburg, sites it high above a tangle of brush, against a backdrop of sky. Protected by the bramble-covered hill, it appears to preside over the surrounding countryside as ceremoniously as did the Parthenon over Athens.

In 2004, Kutz showed a tribute, *Grand View Ship Hotel (A Little Piece of Ship No. 2)*, at the Westmoreland Museum in the exhibition "Along the Lincoln Highway." A Plexiglas plate etched with the form of the Ship Hotel mounted to cast a shadow onto a scavenged piece of the building, the work was simultaneously a hauntingly compassionate evocation and a symbol of the passing of an age.

The familiarity acquired from long-term immersion in a subject translates into an intuition on what to include, how far to push an image, and what would appear jarringly wrong, which subconsciously accompanies Kutz when he's painting and must contribute to the feeling of spontaneity in his works, thoughtful but not overintellectualized, exploratory but true. There is also an aspect

Grand View Ship Hotel
1985, acrylic on canvas, 46 x 48 inches
Westmoreland Museum of American Art, Greensburg, Pennsylvania.

of witness to the events and landscapes that are contemporaneous, but also to that which came before. It is as though the secrets of life and mortality lie within the land Kutz transverses, and if he's able to probe deeply enough, to train his eye to see beyond the immediacy of the moment, he'll be made privy to them.

The Lincoln Highway and its environs are fortunate to have Kevin Kutz as a visual biographer who has given them permanent presence. The oeuvre that he continues to compile is destined to take its place alongside those artworks and archives that collectors and scholars of Americana have valued throughout proceeding centuries.

The Road

McConnellsburg Exit

1982, oil on panel, 12 x 12 inches
Location unknown

It seems the 1970s was a decade for bypasses, even though major traveling was done on the Pennsylvania Turnpike. The increasing population results in more drivers causing traffic jams in little one- and two-stoplight towns like McConnellsburg, designed for horses and wagons, not forty feet of tractor and trailer.

This image has a lot of depth as a result of the perspective, but when looked at as a surface pattern, the road creates an interesting shape. My early pencil drawings had roads in them, and I realized the basic principles of perspective through drawing straight or curved roads. This was a revelation for a kid falling in love with the image.

Route 30 Bypass

1983, oil on canvas, 36 x 60 inches
Collection of C. S. McKee

The Juniata River was shifted to the south at this point near Bedford, though it previously flowed where the present-day bypass was built.

Unsatisfied with this attempt, I returned home and poured turpentine over the whole canvas and started to wipe it out with a rag. The effect it created appealed to me, so I began playing around with it.

Nocturnal Bypass

1985, oil on canvas, 36 x 36 inches
Destroyed

This is a view of the Lincoln, but the drive-in theater on the hill was inspired by one above I-81, north of Scranton. I used the haunting image of movie star Mary Astor on the screen as an ominous viewer watching us instead of us watching her.

Ohio

1998, oil on panel, 24 x 24 inches
Concept Art Gallery, Pittsburgh

The flatter terrain of the Lincoln in Ohio makes the road seem more like a ribbon, to use Woody Guthrie's metaphor.

Similar to the accidental effect created in *Route 30 Bypass*, the turpentine can spilled onto my initial effort and obliterated the image. This act of God and my bouncy truck bed invited me to re-create the scene from memory.

Sun Rise on the Seven Mile Stretch

The Seven Mile Stretch, a c.1938 Curt Teich and Company postcard.

Seven Mile Stretch

2000, oil on canvas, 4 x 12 feet
Private collection

Atop Allegheny Mountain in Somerset, the road flattens out on the plateau. The curves are less frequent. Travelers experience only about five miles of this straight stretch.

In this painting, I wanted to emphasize something vertical on a horizontal format.

Detail of Sunday Drive.

Sunday Drive

1997–2005, oil on twenty panels, 8 x 10 feet
Artist's collection

These panels depict various roadside attractions on or near the Lincoln, several self-portraits, and the people on the road and in my life. After my mother passed away, I went to the cemetery and painted the panel of the robin on the gravestone waiting for earthworms. The rest grew in all directions after that.

This style of painting is similar to that of the Viennese master from Pittsburgh, Henry Koerner, with his dislocated realities painted in beautiful iridescent Cezannesque brush strokes. I was also thinking of Jackson Pollock, only with imagery.

The past twenty-five years have had me standing by the Lincoln Highway, feeling like an idiot while I smeared "colored butter" onto canvas, panel, or paper. Once in a while, I hear someone holler, "Asshole!" More often I get a thumbs-up sign. My road is more than half traveled. I realize I'm not cut out for fame or fortune; I just need to be left alone to work in peace.

The Country

Patchwork

1983, oil on panel, 36 x 36 inches
Collection of Fred Ciocca

In the late 1960s and early 1970s, the Ray's Hill and Sideling Hill Tunnels of the Pennsylvania Turnpike were bypassed and abandoned. The cut in Ray's Hill obliterated any and all remains of Bill's Place, which had sat along the Lincoln Highway since 1923, with thirteen gas pumps, restaurant, souvenir shops, lookout tower, and the "world's smallest" post office.

I painted this view from where Bill's Place used to be. The hills and fields remind me of a giant quilt.

The Quarry Painting

1984, oil on nine canvases, 6 x 6 feet
Collection of Richard Mowry

Now filled in, this quarry located near Mile Level provided stone for early roadbeds. An elderly gent who used to float around on his back in the quarry for hours said that the old steam shovels hit a spring back in the 1920s.

Junk Yard

1985, oil on panel, 32 x 16 inches
Collection of William S. Bartman

Since I painted this, the graveyard of late, late
models in Stoystown, Pennsylvania, has expanded
at least ten times in size, and I think it's just get-
ting started. The owners said I could paint in the
junkyard if the dog didn't get me.

Spring '87

1987, oil on canvas, 28 x 60 inches
Private collection

To this day, the Narrows near Bedford, where all traveling is done through the gap, has been a bottleneck, unless one wishes to hike up over the hills.

Start painting spring in late winter and go back each day to really see a miracle unfold.

Lincoln Highway Farm
1998–99, oil on canvas, 6 x 6 feet
Concept Art Gallery, Pittsburgh

The Ship Hotel stood on the mountain in the background, and down the hill to the left are several cottages once known as Shawnee Cabins. The expanse of the panorama is very wide, so I tried to make the sky as interesting as the land.

As a child, riding in my parents' car, my eyes were glued to the view out the window, mesmerized by the passing dotted lines and bouncing electric wires. Hills, farms, trees, fields, creeks, rivers, barns, junkyards, clotheslines all were eye candy for the ten-year-old who is now fifty. I never lost that fascination.

Mail Pouch

1990–2000, oil on canvas, 8 x 8 feet
Artist's collection

The first painting I ever sold was of a Mail Pouch barn. Eventually I got to meet Harley Warrick, who painted the ads on twenty thousand barns. I've had my eye on this one near Harrisonville for more than twenty years, and it hasn't changed but for a few missing boards.

9/11/03

2003, oil on canvas, 25 x 35 inches
Artist's collection

I was planning to paint this view of a former strip mine near Stoystown the day the planes hit. Needless to say, I was deterred. Flight 93 crashed in the area beyond the two cranes. I went back two years later to paint it. I wonder if that smoke will ever clear.

Jean Bonnet (Four Mile House)

2003, watercolor, 28 x 32 inches
Collection of Shannon and Melissa Jacobs

Jean Bonnet (Morning View)

2003, oil on panel, 24 x 36 inches
Collection of the Jacobs Family

The Jean Bonnet is an old stone tavern at the fork of two roads, originally Indian paths. The road to the left, now State Route 31, was known as the Glade Pike. It leads to Wheeling, West Virginia, where it hits the National Pike and the Ohio River. The other, now U.S. Route 30, was the Forbes Road, which became part of the Lincoln Highway.

The tavern still operates today. Editor Kyle Weaver and I often met at the big, round table in the Washington Room to plan and develop this book.

Bridges

Bridge at Fort Loudon

1982, oil on panel, 12 x 12 inches
Location unknown

This old iron bridge, which crossed Little Cono-
cocheague, replaced an older iron bridge in 1924.
They've both since been replaced with a new concrete job.

Columbia/Wrightsville Bridge

1983, oil on panel, 10 x 48 inches
Collection of Mary and Zack Vlahos

I painted this bridge, with its twenty-seven arches spanning a river one mile wide, at twilight.

In the eighteenth century, a ferry crossed the Susquehanna at this location. A bridge was built in 1812, and another replaced it in 1832. The second bridge was burned in 1863, during the Civil War, to prevent Confederates from advancing in the Gettysburg Campaign. The old stone piers from a steel truss that was built in 1897 and destroyed in 1964 are still visible.

Remains of the Narrows Bridge behind the new bridge, 2005.

Fall of '84

1984, oil on canvas, 24 x 60 inches
Collection of Ruth Fisher

The Narrows Bridge, built in 1934, crosses the Raystown Branch of the Juniata near Bedford and is said to be the first concrete-arch bridge constructed for highway use. It has been dismantled down to the arches and is to be reconstructed. This view from the southwest now has been obstructed by the new eastbound bridge.

A design consultant in Pittsburgh had me change this painting four times, until she finally liked it. Then she bought a different painting.

Narrows Bridge over Raystown Branch, Juniata River, East of Bedford

The Narrows Bridge, a c.1938 Curt Teich and Company postcard.

Spring '86

1986, oil on canvas, 24 x 60 inches
Collection of C. S. McKee

The bridge I have painted most often is the Narrows. It is not straight and level, but is curved and ascends east to west.

A young composer named Todd Goodman wrote a symphony called *Sketches of Home*, which debuted in March 2005 and includes a movement about the Narrows Bridge. Goodman said he was inspired by my paintings. I took that as the ultimate compliment.

Westinghouse Bridge, a c.1938 Curt Teich and Company postcard.

Westinghouse Bridge

1988–89, charcoal, 24 x 60 inches
HighMark Blue Cross

In the mid-1980s, I shot black-and-white film of the reconstruction project on the Westinghouse Bridge in East Pittsburgh, but I did not draw it until five years later. The center arch is 465 feet across—a record for that time. Working from a flat photograph, I layered the drawing to emphasize the distance. It may have worked a little. The restoration of this engineering marvel was worth trying to capture.

Red Coat

1988, oil on canvas, 16 x 23 inches
Collection of Joan and John Taylor

I painted this from a spot in Bedford where Lysinger's Mill stood for many years. Well before the mill was built, the grounds housed the home and tavern of Garrett Pendergast, where many a British redcoat found respite by the stone fireplace, so colorfully described by Hervey Allen in his great novel *City in the Dawn*.

I had a dream in which I was painting a bridge and a woman in a red coat walked over it. The next day, I started this painting.

Narrows Bridge Impression

1993–94, oil on canvas, 24 x 36 inches
Southern Alleghenies Foundation

After painting the Narrows Bridge dozens of times in various manners, I came up with this. It is more about color relations than a bridge. The influences of Mark Rothko, Hans Hoffman, and maybe a little Mondrian are apparent here.

Towns and Cities

Pitt Street

1981–82, oil on panel, 48 x 48 inches
Artist's collection

The front foundations of these buildings in Bedford may have been laid in the dry moat that encircles the original Fort Bedford. Though this is not a confirmed fact, the mystery is there, and I was not aware that the fort was even on this site as I painted from the rooftop of the Ridenougher Building for two years.

41

Street Scene

1983, oil on panel, 16 x 32 inches
Location unknown

I painted this from an old slide taken by Carl Butz. According to his widow, the late Velma Butz, Carl had gone to school only through the third grade, yet he read enough books to become a professional photographer and proof-reader for a Lancaster newspaper.

Bedford Spring

1983, oil on panel, 48 x 48 inches
Ligonier Public Library

My studio is on the top floor of the white building. The red brick building to the right was the Union Hotel, which served as a hospital for injured soldiers during the Civil War. An archway in the basement led to a tunnel under the street and was part of the Underground Railroad, providing sanctuary to runaway slaves.

The Thompson Brothers Carnival left town before I finished the painting, and it never returned.

Farewell Pittsburgh

1985–86, oil on canvas, 6 x 6 feet
William S. Bartman Foundation

A portion of the Lincoln Highway in Pittsburgh, known as the Boulevard of the Allies, descends west out of the Oakland section and becomes one-way. I sort of fell in love with the Allegheny River, but I had too much hick in me to stay in the city. This is a dark, brooding psychological painting.

47

Deatrick's Grocery

1989–91, oil on canvas, 60 x 48 inches
Southern Alleghenies Museum of Art

I never met any of the Deatrick family or had any connection other than a photo of the building I shot in 1981. It was just one of those intriguing facades that had a sense of time preserved from someone's slice of life in the town of St. Thomas.

Sometimes I feel that painting the places I've loved is a last-ditch effort to preserve some piece of it. This is not merely nostalgia, for I am painting the present, which becomes the future's past. Today you can buy a slice of pizza in what used to be Deatrick's Grocery.

Bowman's Dream

1995, oil on canvas, 6 x 6 feet
Wyndham Garden Hotel, Pittsburgh

In the mid-1920s, Dr. John Bowman, then chancellor of the University of Pittsburgh, cranked up his old Victrola and played Richard Wagner's *Die Walkure* for Michael Klouder and his architectural associates, stating that he wanted a building designed relative to the orchestral pieces, with all of its buildup of climax upon climax. This story was relayed to me through one of my mentors, Robert Brackman, who had been commissioned to paint Bowman for the university. The portrait now hangs there along with the architectural drawings and the Wagner-influenced sketches, which are strikingly similar to the completed Cathedral of Learning.

Vertical Vista (Detail)

1998–2000, oil on panel, 7 x 3 feet
Concept Art Gallery, Pittsburgh

Pittsburgh's Forbes Avenue goes through Oakland and then meanders downtown. The Cathedral of Learning, which houses the classrooms for the University of Pittsburgh, appears in the background of many Pittsburgh paintings. From a distance, one can see where Forbes Avenue becomes the Boulevard of the Allies, which was constructed in the 1920s and had been the most expensive highway project to date.

Main Street

2003, oil on panel, 4 x 8 feet
Garden Gallery, Londonderry, Vermont

The town of Everett has a rather honest, unpretentious Main Street. The charmingly quirky retro-Victorian lights often come into the scene when funds are allotted for town revitalizations. People always want it as it was. I paint it as it is, which becomes what it was.

This scene was originally proposed as a mural, but there were fears that people might drive into the building it was to be painted on.

Fort Loudon

2004, oil on panel, 6 x 24 inches
Collection of Gail Czajkowski

Fort Loudon is a beautiful little hamlet to the east of the Appalachian Mountains. In the mid-eighteenth century, this was the west end of the "civilized world." In the early twentieth century, there were some Model T garages on each side of this town. It doesn't need any revitalizing as far as aesthetics go. The reconstructed fort is east of town on the original site.

Gas Stations

Kevin Kutz, 1981: "Cigars helped keep the bugs away."

56

Dunkle's Gulf

1981, oil on panel, 48 x 48 inches
Collection of Jack Dunkle

The design of a painting is intended to be as important as the subject, but with this beauty it is a pretty tough competition. The tan-colored terra-cotta Gulf station was opened in Bedford in 1933 by Dick Dunkle, who ran it until 1975, when his son Jack took over and has been running it ever since. The greatest thing about this place is that it has been run by the same family since it opened—real people I am glad to know.

My depictions of gas stations are celebrations of the places themselves. The true art was done by the designers, architects, and builders. I just stand across the street at my easel, sponge it up, and let it flow out onto the panel. Often I don't even feel as though I am making art.

Mobil

1982, oil on canvas, 30 x 40 inches
Collection of Martha Valentine

The Pegasus has long since flown away, and the Mobil station in Mountville has evolved into a generic box, vaguely appealing to a minimalist.

Calhoun's Atlantic

1983, oil on panel, 4 x 6 feet
Collection of Frank Wrenick

The best part of doing this painting was meeting Ralph "Wild Bill" Calhoun. He said he was given this nickname because he got so many ringers playing horseshoes. Before the Pennsylvania Turnpike was constructed, everyone traveled the Lincoln Highway. Ralph told me the cars in Bedford had to line up for blocks to get gas at the nearby Dunkle's. Then the Calhouns built this Atlantic station, but cars still had to wait. The opening of the turnpike changed all that. The islands remain, as customers park their cars under the 1970s ARCO station overhang to go into what is now Leternt's Pharmacy.

Dunkle's Gulf Watercolor

1992, watercolor, 22 x 34 inches
Collection of Michael Kutz

Before I did this rendition, Jack Dunkle Jr. cleaned the station's exterior, repainted the lettering, and scrubbed the cement joints with a toothbrush.

My dad was sick while I was working on this painting, and I would have to be reached in case he fell and Mom couldn't help. This was before cell phones, so I told her to call either Dunkle's or the house I was painting it from. When my brother rode by on a bike and said, "It's finished," I thought he was referring to my painting.

Texaco

2000, oil on panel, 3 x 4 feet
Artist's collection

In Mansfield, Ohio, I admired the remains of this old station that the present-day water company had preserved. I feel that the paintings I do from photos lack soul. Painting from life allows one to get to the heart of the matter. This is why my stronger paintings are done close to home.

Columbia Amoco

2005, watercolor, 18 x 24 inches
Artist's collection

Sometimes I want a painting to have the quality of a photograph of a memory. This neat, old round-cornered Amoco station was in a batch of slides I took in 1981. It has since been revamped, so I thought I'd try to preserve a memory. It's not really a nostalgic thing. My memory is an element of the present.

Diners and Restaurants

The Coffee Pot at Night

1981, oil on panel, 48 x 48 inches
Collection of Sally Berk

This is a giant Oldenbergian outdoor still life with cars at night in the rain. Pretty crazy! I had painted the Coffee Pot in Bedford six times before I got the nerve to go inside. A few years later, I met my daughter's mother there.

Bob's Diner, c.1948.

Bob's Diner

1982, oil on panel, 48 x 48 inches
Southern Alleghenies Museum of Art

Bob's Diner was built by the Mountain View Dining Car Company of Singac, New Jersey, in 1947. It stood in Columbia for many years. It's gone now but has been resurrected elsewhere. The site today is a not-so-vacant vacant lot. I still have the old postcard Bob gave me in the 1980s, when it was forty years old.

Benji's Diner

1982, watercolor, 10 x 12 inches
Location unknown

This 1955 Kullman is now called Keri's Prospect Diner, but I'll bet a lot of the Columbia locals still call it Benji's. It serves good scrapple, and a nice brick motor court can be seen across the way.

Chester Teapot

1982, ink and wash, 23 x 24 inches

Collection of Brian Butko

Chester Teapot

2004, watercolor, 23 x 24 inches
Collection of Sally Kutz

The Teapot originally was a giant root beer barrel. It was converted into a teapot, with handle and spout, to commemorate the flourishing pottery industry of the town of Chester, West Virginia. As the industry declined, so did the Teapot. One time when I visited, I saw the spout lying on the ground. Some concerned citizens had it moved and restored. The gas station across the street sold me a nice little ceramic replica.

Coffee Pot Panorama

1992, oil on panel, 12 x 26 inches
Private collection

I stood in front of my truck, painting off the hood, which is less conspicuous than setting up an easel. Several times people asked if I was having engine trouble.

Kevin Kutz, 1992.

K&M Restaurant

2000–03, oil on panel, 28 x 36 inches
Collection of Ron Donaghue

Half a block off the Lincoln Highway in Bedford is a nice mom-and-pop restaurant that had been in the same family for decades. It took me twenty years of going there before starting to paint it, and then three more to finish it. When I asked the longtime owner, Gus Sotirokos, what the letters meant, he said, "Ketchup and mustard." Actually, it was Koontz and Murry's. It is now owned and maintained by Tim Gardner.

75

Kutz paints "THE COFFEE POT" on the Coffee Pot, 2004.

Pot Reconstruction

2004, oil on panel, 36 x 48 inches
Artist's collection

The Coffee Pot was built in 1927 and opened as a restaurant in Bedford by Bert Koontz. It later became a bus station and then a bar. It stood empty from 1989 to 2004, deteriorating. Thanks to the persistence of the people of the Lincoln Highway Heritage Corridor and the donating Lashley family, the Coffee Pot was moved to the nearby fairground and restored by a group of college students working for Village Restoration. While I was sketching and painting the progress, a cicada hit me in the eye. It's there in the painting. When the students were done with their job, so was I with mine. I was honored to get to paint the window and door trim, as well as the letters "THE COFFEE POT" on the Pot itself.

Charlie's, the Unfinished Diner

2005, gouach, 14 x 20 inches
Artist's collection

Scotty's, a 1940s National-brand diner in Wilkinsburg, near Pittsburgh, later became Charlie's. It now stands closed.

I did a painting called *Blue Diner*, which appears in Brian Butko and Kevin Patrick's book *Diners of Pennsylvania*. The painting evolved over a two-year period; I finished it the day of Scotty's funeral. Charlie, the cook, took over at the diner for several years. A Saturday morning breakfast at Charlie's was real-life theater. Raphael Soyer said that as his art matured, he'd leave the paintings a little unfinished. I recently painted this version of Charlie's, and I may give it another shot, but for now this is how it is.

Dutch Haven

2005, mono print, 32 x 28 inches
Artist's collection

I was hesitant about painting the Dutch Haven at first—the Pennsylvania Dutch aren't from Holland. But I talked myself into doing it, for it is what it is—a great example of roadside architecture.

cash register told me they weren't for sale but I could have the whole place for $1.9 million. Then the woman working the

DUTCH HAVEN

MONO-TYPE

IT LOOKS AS GOOD AS SHIT

Theaters and Drive-Ins

Lincoln Theater

1982, oil on panel, 48 x 48 inches
Location unknown

This was my first conscious Lincoln Highway painting. The drive-in was a great tribute to the road it was on, as well as to the era, with the opposite colors of orange and blue—hot and cold. The early original orange monolith later had its big blue ears added on the sides to accommodate the larger cinemascope movies of the fifties.

Nothing is left to indicate that a drive-in theater was formerly here. Storage barns and trailer rental lots now prevail. I had some reproductions of the painting with me when I was passing through the area and thought I would plant some seeds. It took me three times driving back and forth on the Lincoln Highway west of York before I felt I had found the metamorphosed place. As the man there inquired of my presence, I held up the print and asked if the drive-in used to be on this site. He verified the fact and expressed interest in purchasing the framed one in the backseat. I gave him a free one with my phone number to call if there were any interested customers. I'm not much of salesman and have told people that "paintin' them is the easy part."

Pitt Theatre in Bedford during renovations, 1981.

The Pitt Theatre

1981, oil on panel, 48 x 48
William S. Bartman Foundation

The Art Deco yellow Vitrolite panels were removed, as was a triangular over-hanging marquee; these were replaced with artificial stones and a flat, rectangular marquee. Rising insurance costs, sign ordinances, and keeping with the Colonial look of the town contributed to the loss. On a happier note, the theater still thrives with one big screen, a nice interior, and a box office.

It was not hard for me to fall for the Art Deco movie theaters after painting the Pitt Theatre. I was under the spell of its geometric patterns and lines. Vintage jazz of that era was the music for my ears. Even though I was an old-time string-band type, I dug those intricate progressions along with the patterns and saw them as congruent to the Deco style.

I painted it from an alley across the street, with flashlight in left hand and paintbrush in right.

Moonlite Drive-In

1989, oil on panel, 12 x 36 inches
Location unknown

This was painted in daylight hours. Later it turned into a nighttime scene, complete with moon and triangular beam of light from the projection booth to the screen.

The original Moonlite was five miles north of Bedford in Cessna, Pennsylvania. Around 1969 or 1970, the New Moonlite was built. Then it was gone in a flash and turned into a development. Someone in one of the new McMansions asked me to paint their house. I said I'd sketch it. The result was so less than half-hearted I could not charge them for it.

Hi-Way Drive-In

1983, oil on panel, 24 x 32 inches
Collection of Judy Summers

Despite rumors that the drive-in is closing, each April the flea markets begin, and it's not long until the projectors get fired up. Just about every red, white, and blue consolidated store and chain surrounds this, the last existing drive-in on Route 30 near Latrobe for two hundred miles east until the Columbia Drive-In. It makes me wonder what developer will target this place.

Hi-Way Drive-In Closed

2004, oil on panel, 11 x 11 inches
Artist's collection

I painted this last winter from my truck. I exhibited it. Then last week, I drove by and noticed the
way the light was hitting the screen—the kind of
iridescent white I recalled —and I put new life in
the thing.

Stony Brook

2004, watercolor and pastel, 5 x 8 inches
Artist's collection

This was actually the sign for the drive-in that had what was then the "world's largest" screen. It is presently being developed into some restaurants and a bank.

Drive-in theaters have always fascinated me, as they cast their own spell, especially the dead ones that have turned into trailer parks or junkyards. The not-so-ancient screen, pulverized by the elements, still stands as a monument to the eras depicted magically on its crackled, chalky white face. A severed metal speaker lies in the gravel, taking a final rest after years of working long summer nights. I have been known, more than once, to pull into dead drive-ins to watch the sun go down.

Anthony Wayne Theater

2004, pastel, 14 x 10 inches
Artist's collection

Back in the 1960s, the letter "J" from "Jerry Lewis" fell off the marquee of the Governor Theatre in Somerset, Pennsylvania, and hit my brother on the head. I followed suit with Mr. Farentino's first initial for this theater in Wayne.

Greater Pittsburgh

2004, watercolor and ink, 19 x 48 inches
Artist's collection

The Warren family had left the waning coal industry and used their equipment to construct several drive-ins over top of previous mine sites. In the mid-1990s, I photographed the five screens up by the drive-in. I returned several months later and shot the same site. I did not really know how to express this other than mere depiction.

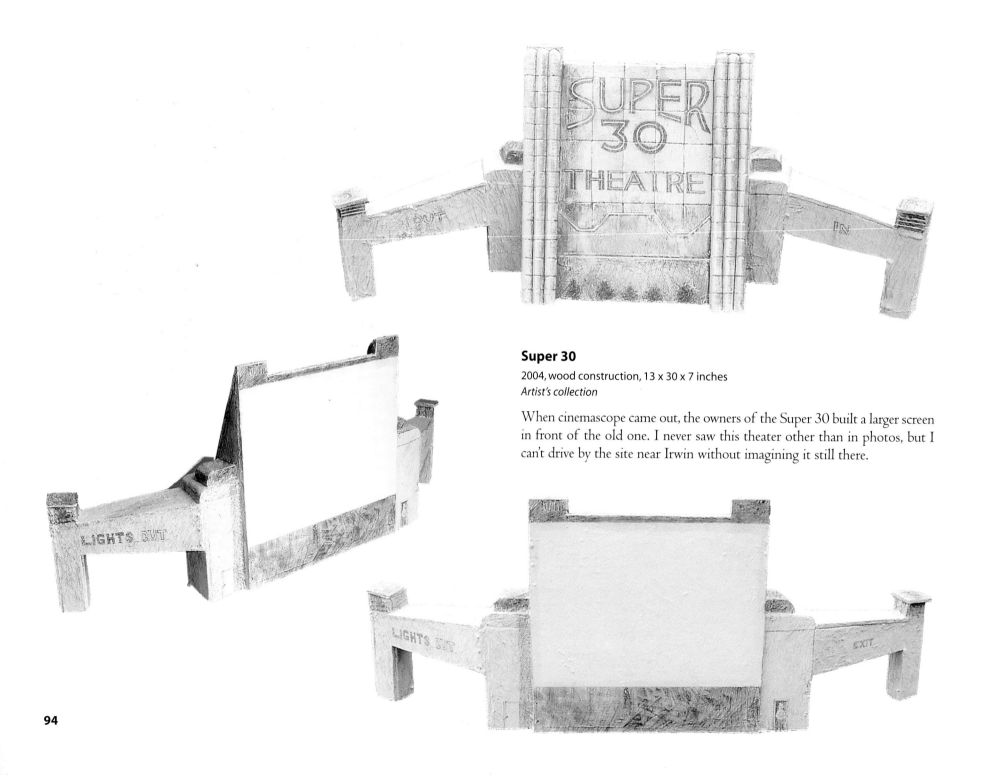

Super 30
2004, wood construction, 13 x 30 x 7 inches
Artist's collection

When cinemascope came out, the owners of the Super 30 built a larger screen in front of the old one. I never saw this theater other than in photos, but I can't drive by the site near Irwin without imagining it still there.

94

Columbia Drive-In

2005, oil on panel, images on both sides, 33 x 48 inches
Artist's collection

The fifty-two-year-old Columbia Drive-In has been purchased by developers. Drive-In fans, known as "ozoners," signed petitions to save the business. Attendance of more than six hundred cars on weekends in the summer of 2005 indicated that the hopes people have are sincere.

My daughter Kate, with her driver's permit, turns into the entrance. We then experience a pleasant evening along with Lucy Beagle.

95

Artist's photos of the Blue Dell.

Blue Dell

2005, ink and watercolor, 19 x 24 inches
Artist's collection

The Blue Dell, west of Irwin, was built from parts and equipment left over from the Super 30, which had been closed and became a shopping center. Though cartoonlike, this is a mind's-eye image that has been circulating around and around in my head for forty years.

97

Amusements

Artist's photo of the Everett Theater box office.

Everett Amusements

1983–84, oil on six canvases, 6 x 7 feet
William S. Bartman Foundation

Joe Grance bought the former Stuckey Theater complex in Everett, Pennsylvania, and maintained it as a theater, boxing ring, bowling alley, bar, restaurant, and apartments. He was one of those local Mr. Wizard types who could not imagine the town without its movie house. I was totally enchanted by the place—maybe obsessed is the right word. Joe and Lily let me paint inside the theater and even turned the sidelights on for me. I felt so privileged. When it came time to decide what to paint on the screen, the Grances' sons, Tom and Jerry, came to mind.

The complex no longer has movies, but the theater is still breathing. It has been converted into a dance area and stage for local rock-and-roll bands.

The Fair Painting

1984–85, oil on canvas, 48 x 60 inches
Gallitan National Bank, Brownsville, Pennsylvania

This painting was done from sketches I made while walking around the Bedford County Fair in the mornings. As I looked behind the scenes, I thought about displacement and the tragic comedy of life.

The Fair Painting Watercolor

2000, watercolor, 18 x 24 inches
Collection of Andrea and William Tarpley

The color, clamor, motion, and sounds of fairs and carnivals make heydays for painters, writers, photographers, and musicians. The authorities came over to see if this guy hiding in the bushes painting a watercolor was a terrorist. I said that I was quite the opposite—I'm a professional tourist.

Story Land

2002–05, oil on panel, 4 x 8 feet
Artist's collection

The members of the Young family, who have been trying to protect their father's fantastic folk art sculptures in Schellsburg, Pennsylvania, from vandals and the elements, have been painting the statues and restricting the property from public trespass. The Pied Piper was constructed in the fifties with wood, chicken wire, and concrete. The Piper's Place recently opened as a gift shop on the grounds.

Story Book

2005, watercolor, 24 x 18 inches
Artist's collection

Story Book Forest was closed for the season that March day when I asked my five-year-old daughter to get out of the car and peek through the opening of the tall wooden fence. I had my camera ready. She did a half pirouette and exclaimed, "Hey! It's a giant book!"

Lodging

Fort Bedford Inn

1984, watercolor, 20 x 11 inches
Collection of Elaine and Jim Housel

Identified in advertisements as "The Pride of the Lincoln Highway" in 1916, this big, old white elephant has been restored for elderly housing. I was afraid it would become a bank or parking lot. I painted it from the inside of a vehicle, as is often the case.

63 MILE VIEW FROM GRAND VIEW POINT HOTEL ON LINCOLN HIGHWAY,

PA.

MD.

W. VA.

GRAND VIEW POINT HOTEL

SEE 3 STATES and 7 COUNTIES

4A-H1905

17 MILES WEST OF BEDFORD, PA. LOOKING INTO 3 STATES AND 7 COUNTIES

Grand View Point Hotel, a c.1938 Curt Teich and Company postcard.

Ship Hotel

1981, oil on panel, 48 x 48 inches
Collection of Ronald Fink

Formerly the Grand View Point Hotel, opened in 1932, the Ship Hotel had its own orchestra. On the wall inside the stern-side windows you see here was a mural of the members, all dressed in sailor suits, with their instruments.

In April 1981, on overcast days, I was up on the mountain standing behind the guardrail, trying for that nautical look. I heard a bear growl from its cage as I painted. The new owners were making the ship into Noah's Ark.

Moonlight Scene of S. S. Grand View Point Ship Hotel, on Lincoln Highway, U. S. 30,

GRAND VIEW POINT HOTEL — SEE 3 STATES and 7 COUNTIES

OB-H1634

17 Miles West of Bedford, Pa.

The Ship Hotel at night, a Curt Teich and Company postcard.

The Velvet Ship

1997, oil on felt, 24 x 36 inches
Collection of Joan DeRose

I'll bet on nights like this, the band was playing. In the seventies, a band known as Wild Turkey played here. The overexuberant crowd led "Noah" to decide not to have any more rock bands.

The Ship Hotel used to sell paintings on velvet, along with a lot of other funky stuff.

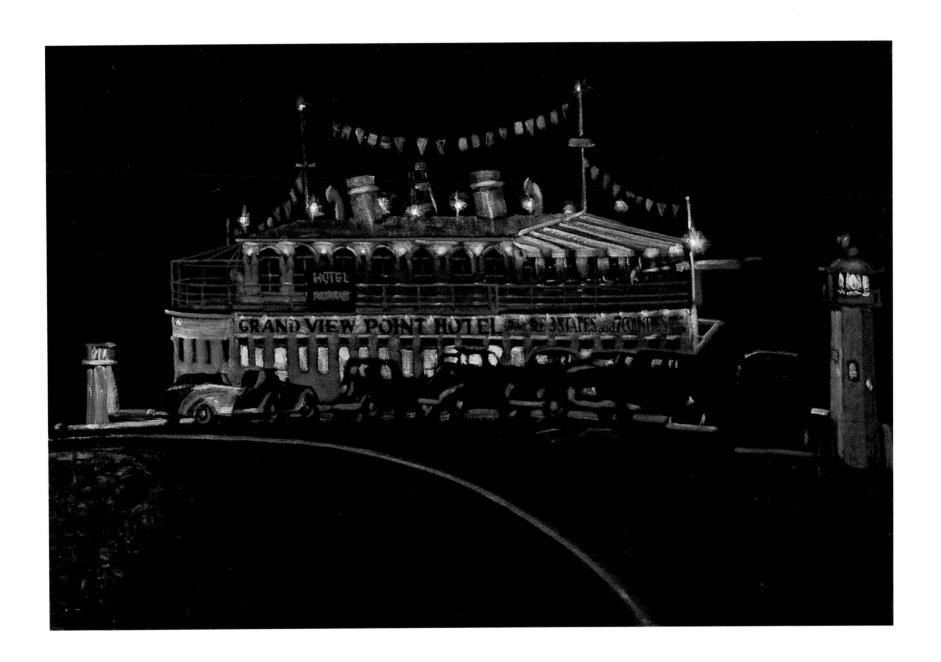

Ship Drawing

1999, graphite on panel, 2 x 6 feet
Collection of Jim Horner

There is something mysterious about looking at old photos. It is intensified when one draws or paints from them.

That's a young Lucille Ball sitting on the back bumper of one of the automobiles. She forgot to sign the register, but Henry Ford, Thomas Edison, George Burns, and Greta Garbo didn't.

Ghost Ship

2001, oil on panel, 12 x 24 inches
Location unknown

Exactly twenty years after my first Ship Hotel painting, I painted it as it was fading in the fog, from my truck across the way. It just seemed kind of ominous to see the much-beloved old girl wither away. Seven months later, it burned down.

Lincoln Motor Court

2001–02, oil on cutout, 12 x 48 inches
Artist's collection

Of all the motor courts that survive along the
Lincoln Highway, this one near Bedford, built in
1944, is the sweetest. I wish I lived farther away
so that I'd have a legitimate excuse to stay there.

Steamboat Hotel

2004, ink drawing, 18 x 24
Artist's collection

This hotel in Lancaster is a nice tribute to Robert Fulton, as well as the spirit and imagination of individuals before the predominance of consolidated chains.

Down East of Lancaster is The Robert Fulton Steam Boat Inn commemorating the inventor of the steam boat who was born nearby. Similar to the late great Ship Hotel in Bedford, this 1991 replica will be a neat place to stay.

kevin kutz

Plywood Motel with Cottages

2005, oil on cutout, 4 x 8 feet
Various collections

Shirey's Motel is west of Ligonier. Bob Shirey said that his family used the money made each year on rentals to build more cottages. All but one of the cottages are gone.

The Haines Shoe House in the early 1950s.

Shoe House

2005, oil on panel, 18 x 36 inches
Collection of Kyle Weaver

The Shoe House is in Hellam Township, near York, Pennsylvania. Col. Mahlon Haines, the "Shoe Wizard," built it in 1948 as a publicity stunt to sell his shoes. His portrait appears in a stained-glass window on the house. In the years since, it has become a popular Lincoln Highway stop.

Twenty years ago, I took a $2 tour of the house. The gal sold me ice cream from the heel and used a skeleton key to unlock the door. "Welcome to the Shoe House," she announced loudly, as if I were a crowd. I looked around and had to chuckle.

Hellam East of York and find Shoehouse
Rond. Billboard beyond read "What are
You Lookin'At?" outdoor advertising.

Pooch came to greet me
Her name was Sox.
A mini shoe in back is a dog box

THE SHOE WIZARD

Ed Sullivan endorsed

Breezewood

2005, oil on velvet, 3 x 5 feet
Artist's collection

As I pondered a game plan of doing a nighttime representation of Breezewood, heralded as the "Town of Motels," I came to realize that the mind's eye was more appropriate in this situation than directly painting on-site. So I gathered visual information, both photographs and studies, and wound up with this image.

Acknowledgments

I've developed an affinity and kinship for the people who designed, built, and maintained the American places along the Lincoln Highway and those who have carried on their legacies. So thanks to Bert Koontz for his Coffee Pot; the Dunkles for their Gulf station; the Warrens for their drive-in theaters; Bob and Debbie Altizer for their loving restoration of the Lincoln Court Motel; Shannon and Melissa Jacobs and their staff for Jean Bonnet Tavern in its present incarnation; the Bob Shirey family for their motel; Joe and Lillian Grance, and their sons Tom and Jerry, for their amusements in Everett; Ralph Calhoun for his Atlantic station; Col. Mahlon Haines for his Shoe House; Bob for his diner; Bill for his place; the Sotirokos family for the K&M Restaurant; Herbert Paulson for his Ship Hotel, and those who took the helm afterward, including Noah; all the bridge builders and road crews; Helen McLaughlin for the Orchard White House; Brian Butko for his thorough documentation of the Lincoln Highway; Kyle Weaver for developing and editing this book and others on the Lincoln and roadside attractions; Kevin Patrick for his work mapping out the historic Lincoln Highway; Bernie Heisey for sharing his extensive Lincoln Highway postcard collection; Olga Herbert and the folks at the Lincoln Highway Heritage Corridor who keep their part of the highway alive and led the effort to save the Coffee Pot; John Beamer and those who pitched in a buck to help save the Pot; Wayne Fetro for his murals; gallery directors at Blue Sky Gallery and Concept Art Gallery in Pittsburgh and Garden Cafe and Gallery in Londonderry, Vermont, for displaying my art; Todd Goodman for his symphony *Sketches of Home*, with movements on the Narrows Bridge, Pitt Street, and the Coffee Pot; my daughter Kate, who rode along and read portions of Butko's *The Lincoln Highway: Pennsylvania Traveler's Guide*, making little rediscoveries and tolerating Dad saying over and over, "That used to be a gas station"; my mom, dad, brother, and sister for sharing auto travels in the early years; my friends, who usually don't know what I'm up to; and my wife and her family, the Slicks and McDevitts, who are true roadside entrepreneurs with their great restaurants, which, had they been along the Lincoln, would have been included in this book; Henry Joy and Carl Fisher for the highway itself; and, of course, Abe Lincoln.

Kevin Kutz